T0025204

MY TINY KITCHEN GARDEN

FELICITY HART

summersdale

MY TINY KITCHEN GARDEN

Copyright © Summersdale Publishers Ltd, 2022

Text by Abi McMahon

An Hachette UK Company
www.hachette.co.uk

Summersdale Publishers Ltd
Part of Octopus Publishing Group Limited
Carmelite House
50 Victoria Embankment
LONDON
EC4Y 0DZ
UK

www.summersdale.com

Printed and bound in China

ISBN: 978-1-80007-347-0

Substantial discounts on bulk quantities of Summersdale books are available to corporations, professional associations and other organizations. For details contact general enquiries: telephone: +44 (0) 1243 771107 or email: enquiries@summersdale.com.

CONTENTS

INTRODUCTION

Welcome to your tiny kitchen garden! Here at tiny-kitchen-garden HQ, we know that gardens come in all shapes and sizes. There are balcony gardens and countertop gardens, gardens that grow up and gardens that grow down. Some gardens grow outside and some grow inside! Sure, some gardens stretch as far as the eye can see, but not all – and when limited space meets the desire to garden, creativity grows.

As William Shakespeare once said about your tiny kitchen garden, "Though she be but little, she is fierce". Little gardens can pack big flavour punches. The secret is simply picking the right plants for your allocated area. This book will guide you through growing to suit your space and your taste. The tips will help get you started and assist those who have mastered the basics but want to learn the next steps.

Most importantly, this book will cover the most enjoyable aspects of kitchen gardening: growing creatively and nourishing your soul while you nourish your body.

GREEN IS GOOD

Why garden? It's hard to describe the joy – and peace – to be found in eating home-grown produce. Does it come from seeing something flourish under your care? Is it from the mix of precision and creativity required for a successful garden? Is it from living more slowly, reducing your carbon footprint? Perhaps it's based in the drive to eat more healthily, and the fact that fruit and vegetables grown by your own fair hand are altogether more palatable. All we know is... green is good!

HOME-GROWN IS HEALTHY

Some prospective tiny kitchen gardeners may already love fruits and vegetables – so they'll be pleased to know that the produce grown in their own gardens will surpass the mouth-watering goods they already enjoy.

However, some may feel more sceptical about the merits of home-grown fruit and vegetables over their shop-bought counterparts. Good news! Home-grown produce tastes better than shop-bought and many find that it is more fun to cook with. One US study found that households that grow their own consume 40 per cent more fruit and vegetables than those that do not. This could be because there is a real satisfaction in cooking and eating goods that you've grown from seed – completing the life cycle you started. It could also be because, when you've put all that effort into growing, you want to create the best dishes possible to show off the textures and flavours.

Whatever the reason, it's possible to grow your way into healthier habits through your tiny kitchen garden.

GARDENING FOR THE MIND

Although you may not feel soothed when the pests have nibbled your seedlings, gardening is a proven way to reduce stress and improve your mood, as it's a mindful activity. It's slow and purposeful – you can't rush a seedling or force fruit to ripen. Instead, you have to engage with the world in front of you, just as it is. You must use all your senses – feel the cool soil under your fingertips, smell the fragrance of the tomato plant after you pinch off a shoot, taste the sweet-sour berry bursting on your tongue, listen to the fall of water from the watering can and look upon the bounty you have grown.

Studies show that it only takes a few plants for humans to feel the stress-reduction effects, so you don't need a forest to lift your spirits. A very tiny garden will do the trick... a very tiny kitchen garden perhaps.

GARDENING FOR THE PLANET

If you're seeking a sustainable life, growing your own may just be one way to do it. Fresh fruit and vegetables – perfectly shaped and sized – are highly accessible, and many previously seasonal crops are now available year-round. But abundance has a high price tag. Many of the crops we find on the shelves have been grown abroad and flown or shipped to their locations, and this process generates a large amount of greenhouse gases. By growing your own food, even if it only forms a small portion of your diet, you reduce your personal carbon footprint.

Growing your own is also a great way to learn to love the imperfect fruit and veg in your life. Around a third of all food grown globally goes on to be wasted – never reaching tables or plates. Once you start producing your own mini harvests, you'll realize that ugly food is still full of flavour and love.

READY, SET, GROW

This chapter will help you equip yourself with the essentials for indoor and outdoor gardening – and show you how to source most items cheaply or for free. It will also tell you everything you need to know about assessing your space and optimizing it for your future plants.

THE GARDENING ESSENTIALS

If you don't have a lot of growing space, chances are you may not have a lot of storage for equipment. That's just fine. All you need to get started is a pot, some soil and seeds. And sometimes not even that – one plant in this book requires only a jar! Here are some essentials that can be bought or crafted:

Plant pots

Pots with drainage at the bottom can be picked up cheaply or for free on local community sites. If you're growing inside you'll need something underneath your pots to catch any water leakage or stray soil, so acquire a tray – old crockery will do – or indoor plant pots.

Seedling trays

Segmented seedling trays with clear coverings are great for nourishing young plant life. *Many* items can be recycled into seedling trays, including cardboard egg cartons and toilet-roll tubes. Plastic bags or wrap can be used in place of the coverings.

Small trowel

Hand trowels come in a variety of sizes, right down to the charmingly tiny. Small-plot holders and container gardeners will likely need at least a standard-sized trowel and fork (unless you subscribe to the no-dig method – a theory that soil quality is improved by not digging or turning the earth). Indoor gardeners who aren't afraid to get their hands dirty might be satisfied using only their fingers.

Watering can and mister

Watering is quite a delicate art. Some plants are very thirsty and others are very particular about when and where they receive their water. A standard watering can with a rose head is a gardening stalwart. However, you may also require a thin-necked can or mister for precision watering. It's the capacity of watering cans that make them such a benefit – gardeners who don't fear repeat trips to the water source can simply, but carefully, use a glass.

TOP TIPS FOR INDOOR GARDENING

Many plants can thrive indoors, under the right conditions. In fact, depending on your climate, some plants may prefer it. A sunny spot under a lot of glass may suit "hothouse" plants, such as chillies, better than a temperate, blustery or cool climate. The key is knowing your space. Before you choose a plant, set up a thermometer and record the temperature at different times of day, including at night, so you know the average conditions in your chosen area. Well-prepared gardeners may also like to photograph the room throughout the day in order to get a good idea of light levels.

Sunshine

Sunshine is necessary food to a plant. A successful growing space needs to have some natural light. The longer and more directly the sun shines on your growing space, the warmer the space will be. This suits some plants but not all – assess your space to learn which plants will thrive there.

- **Partial sun, medium warmth:** "Room temperature" ranges from 22°C (72°F) to 24°C (74°F). This is the temperature that most humans feel comfortable at (experiences may vary – we see you, oh permanently frozen or overheated ones). This is also, generally, the temperature that most indoor plants are happy with.

- **Sunny and hot:** Some plants, such as chillies and peppers, prefer hotter environments. Well-insulated conservatories or lean-tos, with a sunny aspect, can be a happy home for your sun-loving plants.

- **Cool and shady:** Is there any hope for would-be gardeners with plenty of growing space in cooler rooms? There sure is! Some plants have delicate leaves and need to be shielded from direct sunlight.

Eco Pots

The more you experiment, the more pots you'll need. This is the perfect opportunity to repurpose some would-be waste and save money at the same time.

If you have spare newspaper, roll or fold a double layer into a small seedling pot shape.

Cardboard egg cartons are another classic alternative to seedling trays, which are used to germinate seeds before you plant them. As they are already segmented, you don't even have to transfer the seedlings once they have sprouted. Simply plant the carton segment in the pot, plot or bed. The carton will decompose and your plant will grow.

One item you're almost guaranteed to have a regular supply of is cardboard toilet-roll centres. Pack them closely together in a tray and fill with soil, or tape a paper base to them to create free-standing pots.

TOP TIPS FOR OUTDOOR GARDENING

There's plenty to take into consideration when growing outside. But don't feel overwhelmed – a little bit of research and some careful observation will set you on the road to success.

Direction

The direction of your outdoor space makes a big difference to the amount of sun your plants will receive. Some plants require a certain amount of direct sunlight in order to flourish, so it's important to know what to plant where. South-facing gardens will get the most sunlight throughout the day, while east-facing gardens will get mostly morning sun, and west-facing gardens mostly afternoon sun. North-facing gardens tend to be quite shady. Photograph your garden throughout the day to learn where the sunlight falls and when.

Soil

Investigate the soil local to the area if you want to plant directly into the ground. Plants react differently to different soil types. Sandy soil warms up quickly, which is good for planting, but dries out quickly, which is bad for plants. Meanwhile, clay soil is high in nutrients but, challengingly, gets waterlogged in winter and dry in summer. Every soil has its advantages and disadvantages.

Think local

Learn about the kinds of crops and plants that flourish in your local area. This will give you a head start on finding the right plants for your space.

Stay sheltered

Construct windbreaks for outdoor spaces prone to high winds; these could be in coastal areas, on hilltops or exposed balconies. High winds can break fragile young stems and cause fruit to tumble to the ground.

Symbiotic plants

Not every plant grown in a kitchen garden must end up on your table. Planting flowers, such as local wildflowers, can attract bees and butterflies to your garden, who will then pollinate your fruit and veg and increase your crop. Other plants, such as French marigolds, are good "sacrificial" plants. Plant these to lure pests such as snails away from your harvest.

Bountiful but not overburdened

Be careful of overloading structures. If you have a balcony, learn, if you can, the maximum weight it's designed for. Plants get heavy, especially when the soil is loaded with water and the plants are loaded with produce. Be careful, too, of packing hanging baskets or trellises attached to outdoor walls – spread the burden where possible.

Big butts

Outdoor plants prefer to be watered by rainwater rather than tap water, so, if you have the space, set up a water-collection system. Buckets are a rudimentary way to catch rainwater. You can also purchase water butts or siphon water off drainpipes (though be careful not to tap into sewage pipes).

GARDENING IN SMALL SPACES

When growing in a plot of limited size, such as a container or raised bed, you need to consider your space: you can only fit so many space-hungry plants such as courgettes/zucchini into one container. But space isn't the only resource to consider. Co-planting is all about complementary but not identical plants. You'll harvest a greater variety of crops if you consider how the plants use the space: cordon tomatoes grow upwards, radishes grow just under and on top of the soil and carrots grow underneath the soil. Each plant is using a different area of the mini plot, so you can make the most of your growing area.

The other element to consider is seasonality. Perennial plants, such as strawberries, stay in the ground all year long but only produce fruit for one season. However, tomatoes, radishes and carrots can all be grown from spring to summer. Match your crops' seasonality and refresh your bed with new seasonal plants mid-year to maximize productivity.

TINY-KITCHEN-GARDEN DICTIONARY

New gardeners may not be aware of some of the terminology used in space-optimizing gardening. Here are some of the terms that will crop up regularly throughout this book.

- **Caned/staked**: Caning or staking a plant is to tie it to a support structure, usually a bamboo cane.

- **Container gardening**: You may know containers as plant pots. Containers can also be tubs, buckets and trenches. Container gardening is the perfect way to introduce fertile ground to areas such as balconies or paved gardens.

- **Cut-and-come-again**: A "cut-and-come-again" plant is a plant that will continue producing leaves as long as you

harvest cautiously, such as chives or rocket. Cut the outside leaves, close to the base, and only take one or two at a time, giving the plant time to recuperate.

- **Direct sow**: Sowing seeds directly into the soil where you intend the plant to grow.

- **Net**: Covering a plant or tree in a fine net, secured at the sides. Sunlight and water can penetrate the net but pests – including birds – can't.

- **Propagation**: Growing seeds to seedlings in trays or pots.

- **Raised bed**: A raised bed is a small, self-contained plot created by filling a wooden box (usually a square or rectangle) with soil. As with containers, they are a great way to introduce fertile ground into limited and inhospitable space.

- **Repeat sow**: Sowing a couple of seeds every few weeks to stagger your crop. This is a good approach for tiny kitchen gardens that are feeding one person or small families.

- **Vertical gardening**: Growing upwards or downwards instead of horizontally. Floor space fills quickly with pots and plants, so savvy space-conscious gardeners take advantage of climbing or trailing plants.

STYLING
YOUR PLANTS

If there is room for a garden, there is room for beauty. Tiny kitchen gardens can be styled like a microcosm of a traditional garden or take on an air of unconventional bonhomie – it's up to you. Here are some crafts and makes to help you style your garden just how you like it.

COCONUT POT

Coconut pots have a lot going for them. Their natural texture brings subtle visual interest, while they're also a perfect eco-friendly upcycle. Smaller coconut shells are perfect for microgreens and salad leaves.

You'll need:

- Half a coconut shell
- Hand drill
- Four 75-cm (30-in.) lengths of string, knotted at one end
- A keyring hoop
- Waterproof mat (optional)

Method:

Step 1: Drill two holes on each side of the coconut shell, about 0.5 cm (¼ in.) underneath the rim (four in total), and one in the centre.

Step 2: Thread a piece of string through each of the four side holes.

Step 3: Fill the shell with soil and plant your seeds or seedlings.

Step 4: Gather the strings and tie to the keyring hoop, which can be hung on a convenient hook. The centre hole is for drainage so you may need to place a waterproof mat underneath the hanging pot to protect your floor. Alternatively, hang your plant outside.

MACRAMÉ

Macramé is an excellent craft. Once you've mastered just a few knots you have the base skills to create diverse and lovely designs. Plus, with minimal cutting or adhesions involved, the pressure is off. Mistakes can easily be rectified and designs can be reworked until you're truly happy.

You'll need:

- Scissors
- Long, thin cotton yarn or hemp rope
- A 5-cm (2-in.) wooden ring

Method:

Step 1: Cut three pieces of rope so that they measure 1.4 m (55 in.) each.

Step 2: Bunch together the pieces of rope and fold in half. Take the mid-point of the rope bunch (the "loop") and pull it a little way through the ring. Then take the loose ends of rope and pull them through the loop. Tighten the knot against the ring.

Step 3: Starting 20 cm (8 in.) down from the ring, take two loose ends, tie a half knot, and then tie another half knot in the opposite direction. Pull from each side to secure the knot. Repeat twice more with the four remaining loose ends.

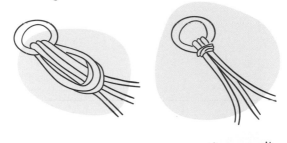

Step 4: Moving 8 cm (3 in.) down from your row of knots, tie another series of three.

Step 5: Finally, 10 cm (4 in.) down from your second series of knots, gather all six ropes together and tie into one large knot.

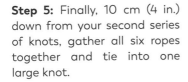

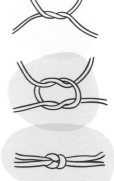

Step 6: Trim the rope and hang from ceiling hook or no-nail plant hanger (page 26).

NO-NAIL HANGING PLANTS

Vertical space is premium plant-growing real estate. But there are plenty of reasons that it may not be feasible to fix planters to your walls: structural weakness, rental property rules, untraceable wiring. This plant hanger is chic, transportable and easy to make.

You'll need:

- A basic clothing rail
- Spray paint (optional)
- Macramé planters (see page 24 to make your own)
- Rope for fastening
- Waterproof mat (optional)

Method:

Step 1: There are many attractive, inexpensive clothing rails available. However, you may like to spray paint yours to add that extra element of personalization. Do so in a well-ventilated room – and choose a PVC-based paint if the rail includes plastic elements. Wait until dry before next steps.

Step 2: Fasten macramé planters to the clothing rail. Hang at different heights to maximize the number of planters. Remember to take into account the eventual length of the plant: place trailing plants in higher positions.

Step 3: If necessary, place a mat underneath the rail to protect your floor against spills and drips.

BRIGHT TIN PLANTERS

Can't find a plant pot in the perfect shade? Make your own! Tins are readily available and this easy upcycle is a way to quickly acquire pots.

You'll need:

- One tin, empty and clean
- Acrylic paints
- Paint brushes of varying sizes

Method:

Step 1: Paint the tin in the base colour of your choice and leave to dry.

Step 2: Use finer brushes to layer detail. A cluster of pots painted in block colour would look very striking. Or you may like to use this opportunity to create graphic prints that you wouldn't easily find in the shops.

Step 3: Once the paint is dry, fill the tin with soil and seeds (or seedlings).

MOSAIC POT

These plant pots have high visual impact but require a little bit of patience. The results are stunning: the mixture of textures and colours will look fabulous against the mixed greens of your tiny kitchen garden.

You'll need:

- Ceramic tiles
- A hammer
- Wooden spatula
- Tile adhesive
- Plant pot
- Round decorative craft mirrors
- Grout powder

Method:

Step 1: Old ceramic tiles can be found for a good price online, at flea markets or in sample packs. Think abstract – a tile that isn't beautiful whole can become beautiful as part of a mosaic. Wrap the tiles in several layers of newspaper and break into pieces with a hammer.

Step 2: Use a wooden spatula to spread an even layer (around 0.5 cm/¼ in. thick) of your adhesive glue over the area of the plant pot that you wish to embellish.

Step 3: Press the tile fragments into the glue. Space them evenly, and allow a small gap between each one (you will grout these gaps). Leave for three hours or until dry.

Step 4: Mix the grout according to the packet instructions. Spread into the gaps between the tile fragments. No need to be overly cautious here, as any grout that gets on the tiles will be cleaned in the next step.

Step 5: Allow the grout to dry for two hours. Wipe the tiles clean of the excess grout using a damp sponge. Leave the pot to dry completely.

UPCYCLED POCKET PLANTERS

This is another craft that maximizes your precious vertical space. Even better, it's two upcycles in one.

You'll need:

- Marker pen
- Empty 1.5- or 2-litre plastic bottle
- Scissors
- Screwdriver or drill
- 1 pair old jeans
- Fabric glue or needle and thread

Method:

Step 1: Mark the point 18 cm (7 in.) above the base of the bottle and draw a line around the bottle at that point, then cut along the line. The base of the bottle is your planter. Drill or punch several drainage holes in the bottom.

Step 2: Measure the bottle planter against the base of one jean leg. Cut 2.5 cm (1 in.) above the top of the planter. You should be left with a denim tube.

Step 3: Turn the jean segment inside out and then glue the bottom together. Press together until dry and turn the "right" side out again.

Step 4: Cut a belt loop from the pair of jeans and glue or sew onto one of the top edges of the planter pocket – you'll use this to hang the pocket, so make sure it's secure.

Step 5: Slip the bottle planter inside the jean planter pocket. If jean material doesn't fit your aesthetic, upcycle other breathable cotton material in the same way.

CANDLE JAR PLANTER

Upcycle empty candle jars once the candle is finished. It's best to use the jars with smoked or coloured glass – too transparent and sunlight may damage your plant's roots.

You'll need:

- An empty candle jar
- A butter knife
- Hot water
- An oven
- Baking tray

Method:

Step 1: The challenge of upcycling candle jars lies in cleaning the jar of wax. There are three options here:

- Scraping: The first method involves a little elbow grease – scrape out as much excess wax as possible using a butter knife.

- Melting with hot water: Pour boiling water into the jar and wait until cool. The heat will melt the wax, which will then rise to the top of the water.

- Melting in the oven: The oven method is a good way to clean several jars at once (as long as they are ovenproof). Preheat an oven to 180°C (350°F). Place the jars on a baking tray and slide into the oven for around 15 minutes. Remove the jars and, holding them using an oven mitt or folded towel, wipe the insides using kitchen paper.

Step 2: Your candle jars are now ready to be used as planters!

PALLET-COLLAR RAISED BED

Pallets are considered good sources of wood for DIY projects. But pallet collars – used to add sides to pallets during transportation – are the perfect way to make raised beds easily.

You'll need:

- Two pallet collars per bed
- Prunings
- Kitchen scraps
- Bag of compost

Method:

Step 1: Stack two pallet collars vertically. This will create a deep, easy-access raised bed. You can keep stacking if you like, but the deeper the bed, the more soil required to fill it. If building on a surface you'd like to protect – for example at a rental property – line the pallet collar with tarpaulin.

Step 2: Part-fill the bed with organic matter such as garden prunings or kitchen scraps usually destined for the compost bin. Lining the base with kitchen scraps will add nutrients to your soil mix.

Step 3: Top the bed with compost. The composition of organic matter and compost should be at least 50:50.

WALLED GARDENS

Some grand houses, and even palaces, enjoy walled gardens. These spacious, carefully controlled environments are pleasing to the eye and feed wealthy residents. Tiny kitchen gardeners will be pleased to know that much can also be achieved with *wall* gardens. If you are blessed with a stone wall there are many plants that would thrive in the nooks and crannies.

You'll need:

- Stone wall
- Thin trowel or knife
- Alpine or hardy plants (The plants you choose should be drought hardy and have shallow roots. Camomile, thyme, lemon verbena, mint, rosemary and lavender all do well in small pockets of soil. You can grow the plants from seeds or use ready-grown specimens.)

Method:

Step 1: Improve growing conditions by burrowing into the soil already in the wall's crevices using a thin trowel or blunt knife, and replacing it with richer soil. You could also add soil to the top of the wall, creating an improvised growing trough.

Step 2: Water your chosen plants well and allow them to drain. Dig space into the newly enriched soil in the wall and insert the plant, compressing the soil around it. Water well.

Step 3: Depending on the angle of the crevice, soil may wash away after heavy rains. Check regularly and top up the soil where necessary.

WEIRD WOOD TRELLIS

This make is one way to add style to an outdoor garden. Trellis is a structure that helps plants to grow vertically, and you might be surprised by the range of materials you can use to create one. Although a wooden lattice is the traditional choice, old bicycle wheels and gates also work well. This weird wood trellis lends your garden a wild, natural feel.

You'll need:

- String
- Three long branches, approx. 2 m (6 ft long) and no more than 2.5–5 cm (1–2 in.) wide
- Six sticks, approx. 30–90 cm (1–3 ft) long

Method:

Step 1: Insert the three long branches into the bed or container where you want to grow your plants.

Step 2: Tie the shorter, thinner sticks horizontally across the branches, evenly spaced. Use the smallest sticks at the bottom and the longest ones at the top of the trellis. Wind the string several times around the points where the sticks and branches intersect, tying tightly.

Step 3: Plant your seeds or seedlings. Plants that grow vertically include tomatoes, squashes and beans.

WHAT TO GROW

There are many factors to consider when deciding what to grow in your tiny kitchen garden: your available space, the light and the heat, the season, the soil and – perhaps most importantly – the food you like to eat. This chapter is full of suggestions to help you get started.

GARDENS HOLD SO
MUCH POTENTIAL POWER
AND THEIR POWER GROWS
WHEN WE TAKE SOME
AND PASS ALONG.

Poppy Okotcha

RADISHES
Outdoor plant

Some people call radishes the "fast food of the vegetable world", but don't hold that against them. Radishes are hardy *and* speedy, plus they're happy to grow directly in the ground, in a raised bed or in a container. If that's not enough, the whole vegetable is edible – and tasty.

- **Growing conditions:** With summer and winter varieties available, radishes can be grown throughout the year. Sow in rows, just a few centimetres apart. The vegetables take only four–six weeks to develop.

- **Top tips:** Seeds can be propagated or sown directly into the ground. Repeat sow every week to stagger your crop – unless you have plans for a mega-batch of radishes.

- **Recipes:** Radish leaves work well in garden salads or even as the base of a pesto. Radishes themselves are a thing of real beauty – peppery bites that can be sliced into thin rounds of contrasting pink and white. Add some pep to miso noodles or a hearty ploughman's with sliced radish.

CHILLIES
Indoor and outdoor plant

Chillies are sun-sponges that need at least six hours of direct sunlight to flourish. Gardeners with warm climates and balconies, courtyards or paved gardens have the upper hand here – the brick and stone create wonderful suntraps. Step out of the ordinary by growing your own chillies – the range of colours and flavours far outpaces the chillies commonly available in shops.

- **Growing conditions:** Sunlight and warmth are the essential ingredients for chillies. Grow in full sun, whether in a sunny outdoor spot or indoors on a bright windowsill. Cane plants when fruit starts to form, as the stems will bow under the weight.

- **Top tips:** Chillies can be picked green or red (or orange or black – there are a rainbow of varieties), depending on your taste. Green chillies have a fresh bite to them while the riper red fruits are sweeter. Hold back on the water for a smaller, but hotter, crop.

- **Recipes:** What recipe doesn't benefit from added chillies? Blitz green chillies with oil, lemon, coriander and salt for a zesty chutney. Include stems when picking chillies and weave or tie together, then hang for DIY dried chillies.

LITTLE GARDEN, BIG IDEAS

ONE MAY THINK OF A
PLANT AS A BRUSH STROKE,
AS A SINGLE STITCH OF
EMBROIDERY; BUT ONE
MUST NEVER FORGET THAT
IT IS A LIVING THING.

ROBERTO BURLE MARX

SUGAR SNAP PEAS
Outdoor plant

Sugar snap peas can be picked at the pea shoot stage or grown until pods form. Both options provide a sweet, nutritious crunch. Sugar snaps are easy to grow as long as you stay alert and protect against pests.

- **Growing conditions:** Plant in grow bags, containers or beds in full sun or partial shade. Sow 5–8 cm (2–3 in.) apart and net well. Pea shoots can also be grown in hanging baskets.

- **Top tips:** Pea shoots can be harvested up to three times by pinching off the tops – the shoots, leaves and tendrils are all edible. Stay on top of the watering if you're growing to pod stage to help the pods bulk out. Cane taller varieties and net to protect.

- **Recipes:** Pea shoots are the perfect addition to a spring and summer salad – combine them with sliced radishes, toasted walnuts and blue cheese. Lightly sauté sugar snaps with butter or garlic and sesame oil for a fresh side dish with bite.

MUNG BEAN SPROUTS
Indoor plant

All you need to grow mung bean sprouts is a shady countertop or a drawer. They are the perfect project for the tiniest of kitchen gardens. As a bonus, they grow fast and are tasty additions to many meals. All hail the tiny but mighty mung bean!

- **Growing conditions:** Mung beans don't even need soil to grow. Simply measure several tablespoons of beans into a jar, cover with muslin or a breathable fabric and fill with water until the beans are covered (pouring through the material). Soak overnight, rinse, refill and repeat over several days. You'll be munching on mung bean sprouts within five–six days.

- **Top tips:** Keep the sprouts at room temperature. Store the growing jar away from the light in order to produce a white bean sprout. Sprouts that are exposed to light gain a green tinge and the flavour alters. Both white and green-tinged sprouts are edible – it's a matter of personal taste.

- **Recipes:** Mung bean sprouts add a tasty crunch to foods such as stir fries and Asian salads. Foodies can also add them to home-made spring rolls.

KEEP GOING,
KEEP GROWING

WHAT
MATTERS IS
THE IMMERSION
OF THE HANDS
IN THE EARTH.

Margaret Atwood

CHIVES
Outdoor plant

Chives are a hardy perennial that never fail to rise to the occasion. They grow abundantly but don't overpower a space. Spring will bring fluffy purple flowers that are – bonus – also edible.

- **Growing conditions:** Chives do best in full sun but are fairly unbothered by partial shade, and are ideal for containers, raised beds or awkward corners of the garden. They'll survive frost and heavy rain but remember to water if you've heavily harvested your crop.
- **Top tips:** Chives are a "cut-and-come-again" plant, which means cutting them back promotes more growth. New growth will take around four weeks to be ready to eat. Pick the flowers when fresh and open – they pack good onion flavour.
- **Recipes:** Potato and chive is a classic combination, as is cheese and chive. Home bakers will get through plenty of chives as they make herby rolls and breads.

CAMOMILE
Indoor and outdoor plant

Camomile is a charming plant that has a jaunty yellow centre and white petals reminiscent of a daisy. The flowers have a "pretty cottage garden" look about them and could be grown simply for decoration. However, they are also easily dried to make tea.

- **Growing conditions:** Camomile is fond of well-drained soil – water once a week if growing indoors and make space for it on your sunny windowsills. If directly sowing, don't cover, as camomile requires light to germinate.

- **Top tips:** Camomile is fairly hardy but it may help to bring outdoor containers indoors during winter to avoid frost. Camomile is a keen self-seeder so, if planting in a bed, be careful it doesn't take over.

- **Recipes:** Pick the flowers and dry on a tray in a sunny room, out of direct sunlight. Alternatively, dry on a low heat in a dehydrator. The more intact the flower, the better tasting the tea.

GO FORTH
AND
PUT DOWN
ROOTS

WORKING IN THE
GARDEN GIVES ME
SOMETHING BEYOND
THE ENJOYMENT OF THE
SENSES. IT GIVES ME
A PROFOUND FEELING
OF INNER PEACE.

RUTH STOUT

LETTUCE
Indoor and outdoor plant

Growing your own salad leaves solves many common salad dilemmas. As it's a cut-and-come-again plant, you only need to pick a handful of leaves at a time, which prevents the curse of the sad bag of salad wilting at the back of the fridge. Plus, home-grown leaves have more crunch and pack more punch than shop-bought ones.

- **Growing conditions:** Grow in full sun or partial shade. Pick regularly to encourage growth.
- **Top tips:** To spread the burden of being eaten, grow several plants and pick the largest leaf from the outside of each. Cut off any long stems and flowers that grow – this indicates that the lettuce has bolted, which means the leaves will taste bitter. Leaves sown indoors are more likely to bolt, so keep a careful eye out, especially during sunny days.
- **Recipes:** Leafy salads are as good as their dressing, whether you prefer balsamic and olive oil or perhaps a squeeze of lemon and a shaving of parmesan. A good burger isn't complete without a leaf or two of perfectly green, perfectly cool, perfectly crunchy lettuce.

ALPINE STRAWBERRIES
Outdoor plant

Alpine strawberries are easy to care for and their small, dark red fruits give the impression of condensed flavour. They're fun too – they can be grown in hanging baskets, cracks in the wall or between paving slabs.

- **Growing conditions:** Alpine strawberries do well in full sun or partial shade. They don't require as much caution as normal strawberries – their vivid fruits bob merrily on the end of their stalks instead of sinking to the ground – but do avoid getting too much water on them as wet fruit will rot.

- **Top tips:** Alpine strawberries are vigorous self-seeders and make for great ground cover. However, plants will tire after three to four years. Propagate new plants from runners – the shoots that grow from mature plants – and replace regularly.

- **Recipes:** Although the fruits can be abundant, they are so small that it can be a challenge to gather enough for a pie or tart. They make excellent decoration in partnership with edible flowers such as violas – and their own small white flowers are edible. Try them on cereal or yoghurt.

HOME IS WHERE
MY PLANTS ARE

NO MATTER
WHAT PLANT,
LEAF UNFURLING
TIME IS REALLY
SO PRECIOUS
FOR ME.

GRETCHEN FULLIDO

SPROUTING BROCCOLI
Outdoor plant

Sprouting broccoli plants are larger than many other tiny-kitchen-garden suggestions. However, they grow over winter and are harvested in spring. Alternate them in a bed with another space-hungry plant, such as courgette, so no growing month is wasted.

- **Growing conditions:** Sow indoors during the summer and grow until the raised bed or container becomes available in autumn. They are full-sun plants, although they are obviously hardy as they do much of their growing over the cooler months.

- **Top tips:** Pigeons are this plant's primary predator – although snails give them a run for their money – so net your broccoli. As plants grow larger they will need to be staked.

- **Recipes:** Lightly roast, transfer to a pan and sauté with soy sauce and sesame oil for an umami hit. Tender leaves can be cooked and eaten as spring greens – they share a rich, mineral flavour with the stems.

KALE
Outdoor plant

Kale is a superfood, rich in minerals and flavour, making it a hero of kitchen gardens everywhere.

- **Growing conditions:** Kale is a large plant that grows well in full sun to partial shade. As with sprouting broccoli, kale can be alternated in a raised bed or container with a summer crop if growing in winter. Kale can also be grown in summer as a cut-and-come-again crop.

- **Top tips:** Stake plants as they grow larger. Kale can be thirsty, so water regularly if grown in summer. Net to protect against birds and other pests. When harvesting, pull from the outside – keeping the central rosette intact will ensure multiple harvests.

- **Recipes:** Kale has a dark, savoury flavour that works exceedingly well in contrast with creamy or sweet flavours. Add to a mac 'n' cheese or serve mushroom and kale tart with a dab of blackcurrant or cranberry sauce. You may be surprised at how well it works.

PROUD
PLANT
PARENT

PEOPLE THOUGHT
I WAS BUILDING
A GARDEN FOR
MAGICAL PURPOSES...
IT DID HAVE MAGIC —
THE MAGIC OF
SURPRISE, THE
TREASURE HUNT.

DEREK JARMAN

NASTURTIUMS
Indoor and outdoor plant

A great choice for gardeners who like a little fun with their functionality, nasturtiums grow in a riot of edible red, orange or yellow flowers, and their broad, circular leaves have an enjoyable peppery flavour.

- **Growing conditions:** Indoor nasturtiums require a sunny windowsill or lean-to. Nasturtiums are an excellent companion plant for a summer raised bed. Depending on the variety, they can climb, creep or trail, so they really will suit your needs.

- **Top tips:** Don't overcrowd your nasturtiums; give them at least 30 cm (12 in.) of space and they will grow to fill the area available. They're not fussy about soil – in fact they are generally hardy plants. Deadhead (i.e. remove the dead flowers) regularly to encourage more flowers.

- **Recipes:** The flowers, leaves and seeds of the nasturtium taste peppery. Add to a salad to give visual interest and a flavour boost. They can even lend their heat to a pesto or hot sauce.

APPLES AND PEARS
Outdoor plant

Fruit trees aren't just for big gardens and orchards. Dwarf varieties of fruit trees such as apples or pears can be grown in large containers. This means that the trees will never grow very tall. Despite this, they crop abundantly.

- **Growing conditions:** Apple and pear trees need full sun to ripen their fruit. They can be vulnerable to frost and wind – if growing on a balcony, consider adding a windbreak to prevent premature fruit-fall.

- **Top tips:** Fruit trees require regular pruning. Don't be scared to cut away at the tree – but research pruning methods first. Young trees need staking and some branches may need support while they produce fruit that's too heavy to handle (if you're lucky). Grow trees in pairs to aid pollination.

- **Recipes:** Fruit eaten fresh from the tree surpasses all shop-bought fruit – there's really nothing else like it. A good crop can be converted into pies or tarts, and savoury fans should consider spicy chutneys.

BASIL
Indoor plant

Basil is widely available in shops, but a homegrown plant can be a bit of a holy grail for amateur gardeners living in temperate climates. Here are some good tips for keeping shop-bought basil going.

- **Growing conditions:** Split the plant into four clumps and repot. House on a sunny windowsill or corner. As with most herbs, ruthlessly cut down any flowers you spot to prevent bolting, as the leaves will become bitter and the plant will die soon after. It will take several weeks for the basil to reach full strength – don't harvest until then.

- **Top tips:** Harvest from the top, cutting above growth. Take just a few sprigs from one pot at a time and allow time for the basil to regrow. Water only when the leaves start to droop to avoid overwatering.

- **Recipes:** Look to Italian cuisine for food where basil is allowed to really shine, such as lemon and basil pasta, caprese salad or bruschetta. In Thai dishes, basil can replace Thai basil when paired with a sprig of mint.

MY BESTIE
IS A PLANT

THE GARDEN
SUGGESTS THERE
MIGHT BE A PLACE
WHERE WE CAN MEET
NATURE HALFWAY.

MICHAEL POLLAN

MINT
Indoor and outdoor plant

If mint had its way, it would take over any garden. Its determination to survive makes it a great herb for beginners. Its natural vigour also means it's a good choice for container gardening – the containers prevent it from dominating your garden.

- **Growing conditions:** A hardy perennial that flourishes in full sun, mint can also thrive in partial shade. Water regularly and pick often – your mint will rise to the occasion. Allow your mint to flower if you like – they grow small white flowers – but picking the blossoms will encourage your mint to grow more leaves.
- **Top tips:** Mint comes in many varieties, both in flavour and appearance. Lemon mint, ginger mint, spearmint and apple mint all have distinct flavours.
- **Recipes:** Grow with parsley and chop together for a herby tabbouleh. Mint is the hero ingredient in many recipes – think mint and pea risotto, mint sauce, mint raita or mint and cucumber water.

PEPPERS/CAPSICUMS
Indoor and outdoor plant

Tiny kitchen gardeners can optimize their sunniest indoor spots by growing sweet peppers. The bright fruits bring joy to the room – and flavour to your dishes.

- **Growing conditions:** Peppers require plenty of sun and plenty of feed. Grow one pepper plant per container and water regularly, opting for a water-retentive soil.

- **Top tips:** Pinch out the growths between stems to encourage better fruit growth. Pepper plants will need caning once the plant starts to fruit. Check your plant regularly to see if it needs further support.

- **Recipes:** Peppers are a mighty all-rounder. Treat yourself to a nibble when raw to enjoy the sweetness and freshness. As for cooking, peppers bring colour and flavour to stir fries, curries, fried rice and fajitas. Make the pepper the star by stuffing halves with herbed and spiced rice.

GROW YOUR OWN WAY

IF YOU LOOK THE RIGHT WAY, YOU CAN SEE THAT THE WHOLE WORLD IS A GARDEN.

Frances Hodgson Burnett

TOMATOES
Indoor and outdoor plant

Fill your suntraps with tomato plants. Cherry tomatoes are a great first plant for newbie gardeners. Once you find your feet, the variations are nearly endless.

- **Growing conditions:** Tomatoes flourish in sunny places and can be planted in grow bags, containers or even summer raised beds. Traditionally, tomato plants make good use of vertical space, but you can also grow bushy varieties. Some tomato varieties are trailing plants, suitable for hanging baskets.

- **Top tips:** Water tomatoes twice a day. Grow cordon tomatoes by staking and pinching out all side shoots, leaving the plant with one strong stem and several trusses of fruit. If keeping side shoots, support with canes as fruit develops.

- **Recipes:** Never fear if you are left with green, unripe tomatoes at the end of the season. Cut into slices and toss in a mixture of breadcrumbs and garlic powder for a tangy side dish.

COURGETTES/ZUCCHINI
Outdoor plant

Courgette plants usually take up a lot of space, but they can be good producers. They flourish over summer, so alternate in a bed with winter crops such as kale or sprouting broccoli. The male courgette flower is edible and absolutely delicious when stuffed.

- **Growing conditions:** Plant out after the last frost in a full sun position. Some courgette varieties climb – opt for these if you'd like to plant courgettes with other plants.

- **Top tips:** Be careful to water under the leaves. Damp leaves can lead to discolouration and mould. As the courgette grows it will come into contact with the ground, so protect against pests. Plants may need caning when young to ensure their first slender stems can support their leaves. Courgettes can be picked at any size, although the smaller the sweeter.

- **Recipes:** Large courgettes can be stuffed while medium ones are perfect for fritters, coated in a crispy parmesan batter. In France they are an essential ingredient in ratatouille, while in Lebanese cuisine courgettes are often stuffed and cooked in yoghurt.

KIND WORDS
HELP ME GROW

EARTH,
I THANK YOU FOR
THE PLEASURE
OF YOUR
LANGUAGE.

ANNE SPENCER

SQUASHES
Outdoor plant

Squash is another plant that needs a lot of space but can be incorporated in tiny gardens using some clever planning. Some varieties can be grown in summer and alternated with winter crops, or you can opt for climbing varieties to companion plant in a bed.

- **Growing conditions:** Grow squashes in a full-sun position. Transfer seedlings or direct sow outside. Squashes can be grown in raised beds or large containers and grow bags. If growing a climbing variety, install a wild wood trellis (page 40) to support the plant as it develops.

- **Top tips:** Winter squashes, such as butternut, can be grown from store-bought squashes. Harvest seeds when the fruit is overripe and then plant them once they have dried. As with courgettes/zucchini, avoid getting leaves damp when watering as they are prone to rot.

- **Recipes:** Butternut squash is the heart of the spicy Peranakan laksa noodle soup, a dish that's hearty and invigorating. Roast a squash and scoop out the flesh to make an autumnal risotto – serve in the skin for drama.

BEETROOTS
Outdoor plant

Another tiny-kitchen treat that is completely edible, beetroots are reasonably quick to reach maturity and can be grown in raised beds with other veggies. They are good, hardy plants for new gardeners.

- **Growing conditions:** Beetroot plants can be grown in full sun or partial shade. Sow directly outside. They prefer fertile, well-drained soil.
- **Top tips:** Sow directly in pairs and thin out (pull the weaker plant from the soil) when plants grow in strength. If eating the leaves, pick a small handful from each plant. Completely stripping the beetroot of its leaves will stop growth.
- **Recipes:** Beetroots are excellent roasted with a sprinkle of herbs and salt, or cooked in a soup. They can also be a surprising ingredient in vegan chocolate cake, imparting an impeccable moistness. And, of course, beetroot is the star of Eastern European soup borscht.

FORMULA FOR HAPPINESS:
X + 1
(X = NUMBER OF PLANTS I OWN)

TO NURTURE A
GARDEN IS TO FEED
NOT JUST THE BODY,
BUT THE SOUL.

ALFRED AUSTIN

FRUIT BUSHES
Outdoor plant

Fruit bushes such as raspberry, blackberry or blueberry grow well in containers. They are perennial, which means the same plant will fruit yearly, but this means you can't use their pot/bed during their "off season".

- **Growing conditions:** Most fruit bushes can be grown in full sun or partial shade. Pick dwarf varieties to ensure the plants are happy in their containers. Grow in pairs – one container for each bush – to encourage pollination.

- **Top tips:** Raspberries require large containers to truly succeed while blueberries are more forgiving. Always check what soil acidity is best for each plant and adjust where necessary. Freshly picked berries are one of life's finest luxuries, so net your bushes to ensure it's you enjoying the fruits of your labour, not the birds.

- **Recipes:** Berries can be blitzed and frozen to create a mouth-watering home-made sorbet. Smoothies are another great way to enjoy the natural sweetness of home-grown fruit. Excess crop can be transformed into jams and syrups – which also make great gifts.

GET READY
TO BLOOM

A BEAUTIFUL PLANT
IS LIKE HAVING A FRIEND
AROUND THE HOUSE.

BETH DITTO

CITRUS TREES
Indoor plant

Oranges, lemons and limes can all be grown indoors, even by gardeners who live in temperate climates. Orangeries – glass-walled rooms housing citrus plants – were historical status symbols. It's time to bring them back!

- **Growing conditions:** Sun is a must and good airflow is a benefit. Citrus trees need a minimum of four hours of direct sun a day. As with any tree or bush destined for a tiny kitchen garden, select a variety grown on dwarf rootstock. Trees can take a few years to grow strong and fruit.
- **Top tips:** Avoid overwatering the soil but keep a mister to hand to keep the leaves moisturized. Use a specialist citrus fertilizer to give your plant a boost – but only twice a year.
- **Recipes:** Squeeze freshly picked lemon or lime over pad thai or pan-fried fish. Orange sauces are popular in many dishes, including duck à l'orange and Asian-inspired orange tofu.

BEANS
Outdoor plant

Runner beans, French beans and broad beans are all great crops for taking advantage of vertical space. Pyramid trellises are the traditional growing method but tiny kitchen gardeners should think outside the box and consider growing beans against a wall or around a doorway.

- **Growing conditions:** Broad beans require full sun while French beans and runner beans can flourish in partial shade. All three varieties of bean can be planted in containers after the last frost. Grow under cover to start and cane as soon as the plants start to climb.

- **Top tips:** Harvest beans regularly while they are tender to encourage growth. Aphids – also known as blackfly – love beans so much that there is a variety known as the black bean aphid. Monitor your beans closely and use your fingers to gently squash or scrape aphids where possible. Some gardeners may choose pesticide-based options.

- **Recipes:** French beans taste good steamed and even better if you then toss them in olive oil, garlic and white wine vinegar and serve as a salad. Shred runner beans or peel broad beans and serve with one or more of the following: lemon, mint, garlic, parmesan or olive oil.

ALWAYS NOURISHING AND FLOURISHING

GARDENERS,
I THINK,
DREAM BIGGER
DREAMS THAN
EMPERORS.

MARY CANTWELL

CHARD
Indoor and outdoor plant

Chard is an excellent tiny-kitchen-garden investment. As a cut-and-come-again plant, this spinach-like leafy vegetable can feed you for months from just one sowing. Sow outdoors during warmer months and indoors during the cooler seasons.

- **Growing conditions:** Chard flourishes in full sun or partial shade. It can take time to develop – up to 16 weeks – but the high yield is worth the wait. Some varieties grow different, brightly coloured stems – opt for these if you like a little colour to your crops.

- **Top tips:** If growing in humid conditions, sow with plenty of space around the plant. This will aid in air circulation and avoid the chard leaves developing patchy mildew. Cover young plants to protect from pests.

- **Recipes:** Chard is delicious sautéed with other vegetables or served in a gratin. Combine with mushroom, squash and feta in a tart or pie for an autumnal dish. Chard also shines in a gingery, garlicky noodle soup.

ROCKET/ARUGULA

Indoor and outdoor plant

Elton John knew what he was talking about when he sang that he was a rocket man. The little leaf is irresistible, packing a big peppery punch. Choose the right variety and you have a quick-growing, cut-and-come-again-crop – perfection.

- **Growing conditions:** Rocket prefers full sun or partial shade, and likes to be well watered. Rocket can resist cool autumn weather but protect it by wrapping the pot in fleece – and grow inside in the winter.
- **Top tips:** Don't let your rocket overheat or get too dry – it will bolt. Repeat sow for a steady supply of leaves, picking a few at a time and moving on to the next plant.
- **Recipes:** Rocket is the superstar of salads, doing a lot of the heavy lifting in terms of flavour. Pretend you are a fancy pizza place by serving up a slice topped with rocket. Or think outside the box and add to home-made fishcakes for a lively kick.

POTATOES
Outdoor plant

You don't need a lot of space to grow potatoes; a couple of deep containers and a position of full sun to partial shade will fit the brief.

- **Growing conditions:** There are generally three types of potato: first earlies, second earlies and main crop. The names refer to when they crop – first earlies are the first to mature, then second, and finally main crop. First and second earlies generally produce smaller new potatoes while main crop is the source of big baking or roasting potatoes and can be stored.

- **Top tips:** Watch out for blight – a dark fungus that can be first identified in the leaves. Once spotted, blight needs to be dealt with quickly; if it travels down to the tubers – the potatoes – they will turn and rot.

- **Recipes:** Potatoes are a hero ingredient – they can be the star on their own or be the perfect side. There's something so special about the delicate, golden first and second earlies. Parboil, lightly crush and roast with rosemary and a crank of salt.

LOVE YOUR LEFTOVERS

Think of growing your garden as good energy. All the love and effort that you put into nurturing your plants goes out into the universe. Some good plant energy comes back to replenish you in the form of herbs, fruits and vegetables. Some good plant energy reaches out to your loved ones via seedlings, cuttings and edible treats. And some good plant energy flows back to the source, as seeds and scraps, ready to begin the joyous cycle again.

HOW TO SAVE AND STORE SEEDS

Seeds can be stored and saved for next season, whether from your own produce or shop-bought fruit and veg.

- **Choose carefully**: Pick seeds from your most successful plants. It is more likely that the plants grown from these seeds will carry forward the positive attributes from their parent plant.
- **Prepare for surprises**: Shop-bought produce is often grown from hybrid plants. This means that plants grown from their seed can take on the characteristics of one or the other of the varieties used to create the hybrid. Your produce may look and taste different from the original produce!
- **Harvest from overripe plants**: Their seeds will be more developed and ready for germination.
- **Store in a cool, dry place**: Seeds should be stored in an airtight container or firmly wrapped in a paper envelope. Don't forget to label your seeds (unless you like to involve mystery-solving in your spring garden routine).

GROWING FOOD FROM SCRAPS AND SEEDS

Tiny kitchen gardeners may have heard of "farm to table". It's time to complete the circle and go "table to farm" as we grow food from scraps and seeds. Although the fruits and vegetables that reach our table have usually been cultivated for size and flavour, rather than their reproductive abilities, there is much that a zero-waste cook and gardener can achieve.

Leeks and spring onions

Regrowing leeks and spring onions is a bit of a magic trick. Leeks and onions are both members of the allium family and the same method can be used to revive them. This trick regrows the white root at the base of the allium. Simply place the base of a leek or spring onion in a clear glass of water and seat on a sunny windowsill. Change the water every second day. You'll have a new leek or spring onion in weeks!

Garlic

Garlic takes its own sweet time to develop. However, as a kitchen staple, it's worth the wait. Plant a clove, point side up, outside in full sun in late autumn. It will take a year until it is ready to harvest. Don't forget to mark where you planted, unless you have an excellent memory or enjoy garlic-based surprises.

Pumpkins and squashes

Save a handful of pumpkin and squash seeds when you scoop out the fleshy insides. Dry, and save for next season. See page 94 for further information on optimizing your squash crop.

Tomatoes

Yes, even tomato seeds can be saved! Harvest the seeds from an overripe tomato and dry. The best method is to lightly wash to remove excess pulp and spread out on a tray. Place in a warm room out of direct sunlight, transfer to a paper envelope once dry and store in a dark space until ready to plant. Label the envelope with the type of tomato to give yourself a head start next planting season. See page 88 for more tips.

Lettuces and bok choy

The allium water method works well for lettuces and bok choy too. Place the base of a head of lettuce or bok choy, cut side up, in a bowl of water. Refresh the water every other day. New leaves will start to form after around two weeks. Once leaves have appeared, use the cut-and-come-again method to harvest.

Potatoes

Seed potatoes are potatoes that have been harvested and allowed to grow overripe, until roots sprout. Sound familiar? Oh yes, those bottom-of-the-cupboard potatoes can be stored and used as seed potatoes. Simply separate from your eating potatoes (lest you confuse them) and plant in spring. For more on potatoes, see page 114.

Celery

Celery so often goes uneaten that it can only be a relief that it can easily be regrown. Cut off the bottom 2 cm (1 in.) of a celery bunch and place the cut-off base in a shallow bowl of water. Keep the tops moist as the sticks grow and a new root system forms. Once new roots are visible, transfer to soil.

Ginger

Like garlic, ginger is another kitchen essential that can be regrown. Soak old ginger in warm water for 12 hours and then plant sideways. Ginger needs space to grow and plenty of sunlight and water. Use a large pot and place on a sunny windowsill.

HOW TO DRY HERBS

Herbs are a real gift to the waste-averse kitchen gardener. They taste as good dried as they do fresh. Plus, they provide an opportunity to get creative. Think signature herb mixes in your pantry; picture sprigs of herbs lining your kitchen walls; imagine foodie gifts topped with a home-made bouquet garni. Oh yes!

Thoroughly prepare your herbs ahead of drying them. Cut when still full of vigour and wash, gently finger combing to dislodge insect passengers.

- **Air-dry herbs in bunches.** Tie herbs at one end using string and hang in a warm and dry room, out of direct sunlight. Time required to dry will vary. This method works well for many herbs but is particularly good for woody herbs such as rosemary or thyme.

- **Tray drying.** This is another air-dry method which is particularly good for broad-leaved herbs such as mint or basil. Remove the leaves from the stems and lay on a (preferably mesh) tray. Avoid direct sun and busy areas – trays are easily overturned.

- **Dehydrate herb leaves.** Dangling herb bouquets and scattered trays of herbs are charming and aromatic but occasionally inconvenient. If you're experiencing a high herb turnover, consider investing in a dehydrator. These devices will heat your herbs low and slow – but quicker than the sun – taking your herbs from garden to garni in under a day.

LAST WORD

Now you've learned the basics, it's time to collaborate with your garden to get the best results. You know best where the light falls and the shade steals in. And only your garden can tell you the quality of the soil and which plants it prefers to grow. You can use the tips and tricks you've learned in these pages to suggest new plants and planters to your garden – part of the fun is learning what will make it come alive.

For every garden dream that doesn't come true there's an unexpected flash of beauty or a glut of crops. Gardens are about hope, learning and, above all, growth of all kinds. Good luck on your big tiny-kitchen adventure.

A GARDEN MUST
COMBINE THE POETIC
AND THE MYSTERIOUS
WITH A FEELING OF
SERENITY AND JOY.

LUIS BARRAGÁN

PLANT INDEX

Outdoor plants

Indoor plants

Indoor and outdoor plants

IMAGE CREDITS

Have you enjoyed this book?

If so, find us on Facebook at
Summersdale Publishers, on Twitter at
@Summersdale and on Instagram at
@summersdalebooks and get in touch.

We'd love to hear from you!

www.summersdale.com